Songbirds

THE LANGUAGE OF SONG

Songbirds

THE LANGUAGE OF SONG

A Carolrhoda Nature Watch Book

by Sylvia A. Johnson

Carolrhoda Books, Inc. / Minneapolis

To my cousin Peggy Werkmeister, my favorite birdwatcher.

The author would like to thank Frank McKinney, Professor Emeritus, Bell Museum of Natural History, University of Minnesota, for his assistance with this book. I would also like to acknowledge my debt to Bird Song: Biological Themes and Variations, *by C. K. Catchpole and P. J. B. Slater. This fascinating book was a source of information and inspiration in my research on the language of birdsong.*

Text copyright © 2001 by Sylvia A. Johnson

Carolrhoda Books, Inc.
A division of Lerner Publishing Group
241 First Avenue North
Minneapolis, MN 55401 U.S.A.

Website address: www.lernerbooks.com

LIBRARY OF CONGRESS CATALOGING-IN-PUBLICATION DATA

Johnson, Sylvia A.
    Songbirds: the language of song / by Sylvia A. Johnson
        p. cm.—(A Carolrhoda nature watch book.)
    Includes index.
    Summary: Introduces the phenomenon of birdsong, explains how and why birds sing, describes how scientists learn about bird communication, and indicates the dangers to songbirds due to changes in their habitats.
        ISBN 1-57505-483-3 (lib. bdg. : alk. paper)
        1. Birdsongs—Juvenile literature. 2. Songbirds—Vocalization—Juvenile literature. 3. Songbirds—Juvenile literature. [1. Birdsongs. 2. Songbirds]
    I. Title. II. Series.
    QL698.5.J64 2001
    598.8—dc21   99-050533

Manufactured in the United States of America
1 2 3 4 5 6 - JR - 06 05 04 03 02 01

CONTENTS

Singers in the Garden   7

The Basics of Birdsong   8

Studying Songbirds   11

The Singers and Their Songs   14

Learning to Sing   18

Why Birds Sing   27

The Language of Song   42

Songbirds in Danger   43

Glossary   46

Index   47

SINGERS IN THE GARDEN

"*FEE-bee, FEE-bee, FEE-bee, FEE-bee.*" Did you ever hear this sweet song in your garden on a spring morning? Or maybe a cheerful "*Birdy, birdy, birdy*" brightened your spirits on a cold winter day. While walking through the woods, have you stopped to listen to the haunting sound of "*EE-oh-lay, EE-oh-lay*" echoing through the trees?

If you have had these experiences or others like them, then you are one of the millions of people who are fascinated by the songs of birds. Like many of these people, you may have tried to find out more about the hidden singers in your garden. Perhaps you looked at a field guide, a book that helps people identify birds by their appearance and song. The guide would have told you that black-capped chickadees say "*FEE-bee,*" that part of the cardinal's song sounds like "*Birdy, birdy, birdy,*" and that "*EE-oh-lay*" is the song of the wood thrush.

Of course, these words and phrases represent what the birds' songs sound like to human ears. But have you ever wondered how the songs sound to other birds? What are the singers in the woods and garden really saying?

THE BASICS OF BIRDSONG

Scientists around the world are also fascinated by songbirds. These researchers, called **ornithologists** (or-nih-THAHL-uh-jists), have some of the same questions about birds that nonscientists do. They want to know why birds sing and what their songs mean. They also want to know how those small, feathered bodies can produce such amazing sounds.

Ornithologists have understood some of the basic facts about birdsong for many years. For one thing, they have known that not all birds are songbirds. A few, such as the stork, make hardly any sounds at all. Many other birds make only short, simple sounds, or **calls.**

About 5,000 **species,** or kinds, of birds produce longer, more complex sounds that often remind us of human music. We commonly refer to these birds as songbirds, or **oscines** (AHS-ines). Most oscines belong to the large group of perching birds, or **passerines** (PAS-uhr-ines), which includes more than half of all living birds.

Perching birds such as this great kiskadee have feet adapted for gripping branches, with three toes pointing forward and one backward.

The song of the blue jay (inset) *sounds harsh to human ears, while the Baltimore oriole* (right) *sings a sweet, whistling tune. Both birds are considered songbirds.*

Many common North American species are songbirds. Among them are robins, cardinals, chickadees, sparrows, warblers, thrushes, and orioles. Even blue jays and crows, with their harsh, unmusical voices, are members of the group.

Ever since we humans first started listening to birds, we have realized that each species seems to have its own special song. Just as people speak different languages, songbirds sing the songs typical of their own group. The chickadee's *"FEE-bee"* and the cardinal's *"Birdy, birdy, birdy"* are made up of combinations of sounds as distinctive as those of Spanish or English.

Another basic fact about songbirds known for years is that almost all the singers are males. In most species, female birds make calls, but the males are the only ones capable of producing real song.

In addition to knowing these facts, scientists who studied birds in the past had some theories about birdsong. Observing birds in the field, they concluded that the songs they heard were not just beautiful sounds. The birds were not singing for their own entertainment—or for ours. Instead, song played a very real and very important role in their lives. Using the latest scientific equipment, modern ornithologists have proved just how right those early theories were.

The song of the male indigo bunting sounds like "Sweet, sweet." The female of this species, like most female songbirds, does not sing. She is also less colorful than her blue-feathered mate.

10

STUDYING SONGBIRDS

Up until about 40 years ago, ornithologists studying songbirds had only their eyes and ears to rely on. Through observation in the field, they learned to identify different bird songs. They made written records of them, often using phrases like *"FEE-bee"* to represent the sounds. Some scientists even tried using the notes and scales of human music to describe complex songs. Then the development of high-quality portable tape recorders completely changed the study of songbirds.

Ornithologists could take these lightweight recorders with them into forests and fields. With the help of the machines' sensitive microphones, scientists could record a single birdsong or a whole chorus of singers. Back in the laboratory, they could play these tapes again and again and study them along with other information collected in the field.

High-quality tape recorders and sensitive microphones have allowed scientists to make clear recordings of birdsong.

Since the 1950s, recording equipment has become much more advanced. Ornithologists can record birdsong on machines controlled by laptop computers. Equipment in the laboratory has also become much more complicated, and more useful. The most important tool being used to study birdsong is a machine called the **sonograph** (SAHN-uh-graf).

Originally developed in the 1950s, the sonograph breaks a sound down into its basic parts. Sounds are produced when objects vibrate, or move back and forth rapidly. These vibrations travel through the air in the form of invisible waves. A sonograph measures the **frequency** of sound waves—the number of waves that pass a certain point in one second of time. The results are expressed in a kind of "sound picture" called a **sonogram.**

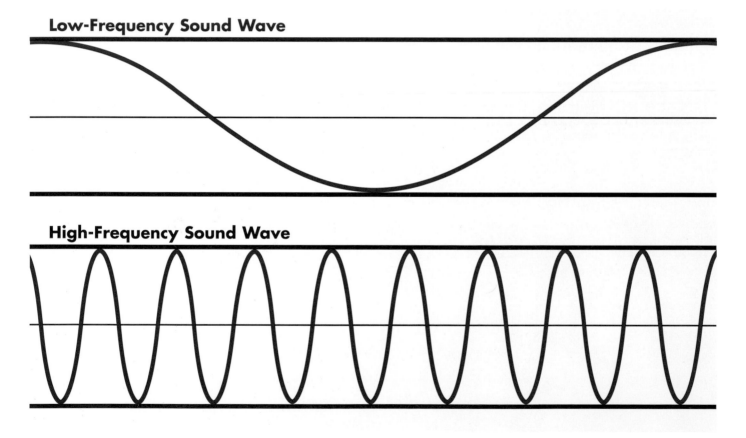

Low-Frequency Sound Wave

High-Frequency Sound Wave

The frequency of a sound wave is the number of waves passing a point in one second of time. A sound with high frequency will have more waves per second than one with a lower frequency. High-pitched sounds—for example, a whistle—have high frequencies. Low-pitched sounds such as thunder have low frequencies.

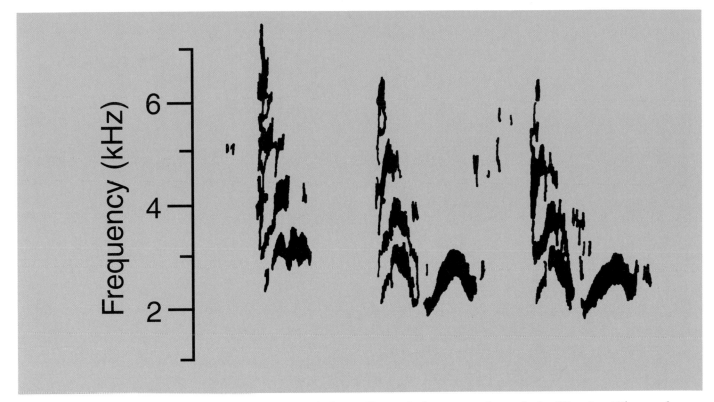

This sonogram gives a "sound picture" of the call made by a species of chaffinch. The scale on the left side shows the frequencies of the sound waves, which are measured in a unit called a kilohertz (kHz).

When ornithologists first played song-bird tapes into sonographs, they discovered an exciting new way to study birdsong. Instead of depending on the human ear to hear the different parts of a song, scientists could actually see the parts displayed in a sonogram. By studying these sound pictures, they could learn a song's exact makeup and structure. They could also compare the songs of different species or of the same species recorded at different times and under different conditions. The use of computers made it possible to compare and study large numbers of sonograms. Soon ornithologists had more information about birdsong than they had ever had in the past.

A champion singer of the bird world, the brown thrasher sings about 2,000 different song types. Some of these songs are borrowed from other species of birds.

THE SINGERS AND THEIR SONGS

One of the most important things that ornithologists have learned is that there is nothing simple about birdsong. It is a very complex natural system that we are just beginning to understand.

For example, while each species of bird seems to have one basic song, sonograms show that there may be many different versions of this song. Scientists call these different versions **song types.**

The brown thrasher, a plain-looking bird that lives in the eastern half of the United States, sings about *2,000* song types. The North American mockingbird has around 150 different types, while the European nightingale can have as many as 300. Even a common backyard songbird such as the cardinal can sing 12 different song types.

The collection of songs that a human singer knows and can perform is called a **repertoire** (REP-uhr-twahr). Scientists use this same French word to refer to the group of song types sung by a bird species. Brown thrashers have a very large repertoire. The ovenbird, on the other hand, has only one song type in its repertoire. This North American species sings *"Teacher, teacher, teacher"* over and over. Another North American bird, the chipping sparrow, also has only one simple song type, from which the bird gets its name.

Chipping sparrows are common birds in many parts of North America. The males sing one simple song, which sounds like "Chip, chip."

15

A marsh wren may have as many as 160 songs in his repertoire.

Studying recordings and sonograms of bird songs led scientists to another fascinating discovery. Different species of birds follow different rules when they "perform" their repertoires. Birds with small repertoires, for example, the western meadowlark, often sing each song type several times before going on to another one. If the bird's repertoire includes song types A, B, and C, it may sing AAAABBBBCCCCAAABBBBCCCC.

At another time, the order may instead be AAACCCCCBBBB.

Some birds have more variety in their singing. They usually sing each song type just once before going on to another. Their song pattern might be ABCDEFG..., or BFDEGH.... Songbirds with large repertoires, for example, the European nightingale, often perform in this way.

Nightingales live throughout Europe, nesting in woods and hedges. They sing their melodic songs during the day as well as at night.

With an average repertoire of 200 song types, the nightingale is one of the most versatile singers in the bird world. It sings each type only once, but it doesn't usually go through its whole repertoire every time it sings. Research has shown that a nightingale performs about 70 of its song versions before starting to repeat songs. Of course, even 70 is a very large number, compared to the single song of the ovenbird or the *"Chip, chip"* of the chipping sparrow.

All the birds in a single species have repertoires of similar size. They also perform their songs in a similar way. But just like humans, individual birds may be different from each other. Some nightingales have larger repertoires than other members of the species. They know more song types and may even have their own special ways of delivering them.

These differences exist because of the way that birds learn to sing. All male songbirds are able to produce songs, but they need "singing lessons" to know exactly how and what to sing. And, just like young people in school, some birds seem to be better learners than others.

17

LEARNING TO SING

Young songbirds hatch from their eggs with all the physical equipment they need to sing. And very special equipment it is. Human beings produce sounds with a larynx, or voice box. Birds use a different kind of sound organ called a **syrinx** (SEER-inks). The syrinx contains membranes (thin layers of tissue) that vibrate when air from the lungs is forced over them. These vibrations produce sound waves. Muscles attached to the syrinx shape and control the sound waves to create all the amazing variety of birdsong.

Mockingbird chicks open their beaks wide, begging for food. Like all young birds, they will need a long training period before they are able to sing.

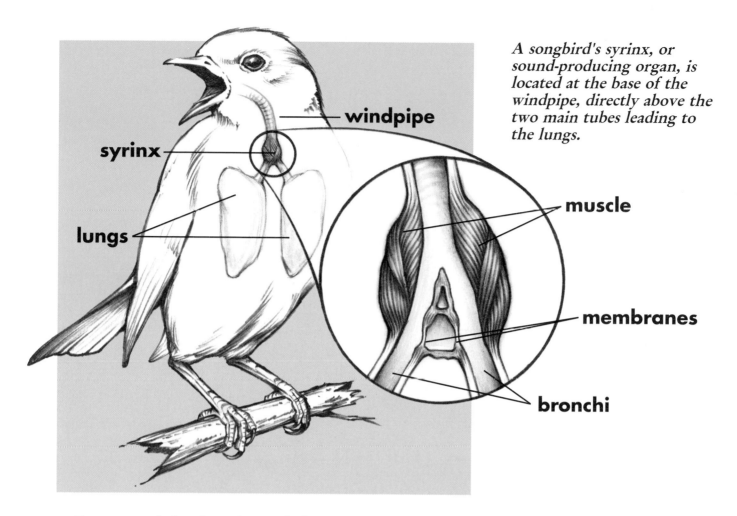

syrinx

windpipe

A songbird's syrinx, or sound-producing organ, is located at the base of the windpipe, directly above the two main tubes leading to the lungs.

lungs

muscle

membranes

bronchi

Because of the location of the syrinx, birds can even sing two different sounds at exactly the same time. The human larynx is located at the top of the windpipe, but the syrinx is much lower down. It is directly above the **bronchi** (BRAHN-kee), the two main tubes that connect the windpipe to the lungs. Air from these two separate sources can produce vibrations in the membranes on both sides of the syrinx. These two sets of vibrations create two separate sounds.

The songbird's special sound-producing system is one of the reasons why bird songs are so complex.

When a young bird first opens its beak and starts to sing, it doesn't produce a complex and perfect song. Like a baby's early attempts at speech, a bird's first songs may sound more like babble than like the songs of adult birds. How a young bird develops the ability to sing the songs of its species is an amazing example of animal learning.

The chaffinch (right), a common bird in Great Britain and Europe, belongs to the same scientific family as the North American goldfinch (inset).

Ornithologists have done a lot of research on this subject, usually by studying young birds raised in captivity. One of the earliest and most important of these studies was done in England during the 1950s. It used a small bird called a chaffinch, a relative of the North American goldfinch. The researchers studied young chaffinches that had hatched out of eggs in a laboratory. None of the birds had ever been in contact with adults of their species. But during the early months of their lives, some birds were allowed to hear tape recordings of adult chaffinches singing.

When all the young male birds were around one year old, they started to sing. The birds that had heard the recordings were able to sing the normal songs of adult chaffinches. Even though they had heard the songs months earlier, these birds were able to remember and reproduce them. The birds in the other group didn't do so well. Their songs were about the right length and sound frequency, but they were very simple and lacked many of the details of normal chaffinch song. These "uneducated" birds were never able to produce the true song of their species.

Since the experiment with chaffinches, ornithologists have studied other birds, including the North American white-crowned sparrow. Most young birds develop their songs in the same way, and learning is an important part of the process.

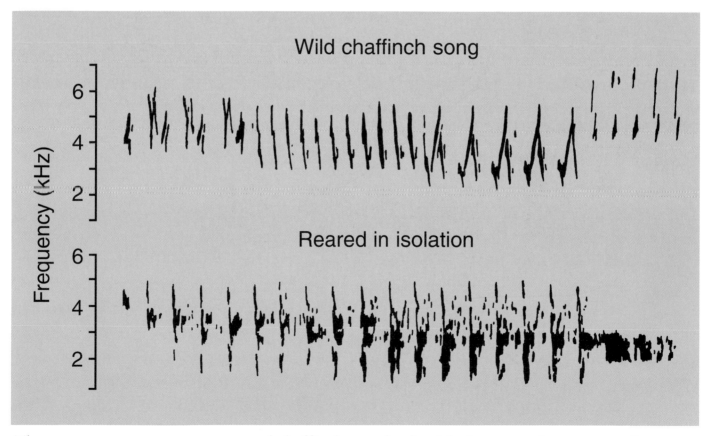

These sonograms compare a normal chaffinch song (top) *with the song of a young male that never heard adult chaffinches singing* (bottom). *As you can see, the song of the "uneducated" bird does not have the clear, orderly pattern of the normal song.*

If these young song sparrows do not have models to copy, they will never be able to sing the complex adult song of their species.

Many scientists think that young birds are born knowing a very crude and simple version of their species' songs. They have a kind of **template**—a guide or pattern—for these songs built into their brains. As the birds grow, they hear the songs of adult males of their species, as well as many other kinds of bird songs. With the help of their built-in templates, the young birds are able to pick out their species' songs. They memorize these songs. Then they use them as models to change their simple templates into patterns for the full adult songs of their species.

Young humans need the example of their parents and other adults in order to progress from baby talk to adult speech. The same is true for young birds. Without adults to copy, most young birds can sing only the crude, simple songs that they knew at birth. No matter how hard they try, they can't produce the complicated sounds of normal adult singing.

The importance of learning helps to explain some of the puzzling things about birdsong. One example is the many variations in the songs of a single species. Since young males learn by hearing different adults, each may pick up the unique features of his "instructor's" songs. Other variations come from mistakes that young birds make in learning their species' songs.

Ornithologists have discovered that whole groups of birds can have special ways of singing. Birds that live in different geographical areas sometimes develop different versions of their species' songs.

Just like human children, young birds learn to sing from the adults that live near them. They copy the adults' singing methods and their particular versions of the species' songs. Such differences are passed down from one generation of birds to the next. Gradually a kind of song "dialect" develops in the area. This version of a song is something like a regional dialect in human speech—for example, the difference between English spoken by people in Georgia and in Maine. The basic song is the same, but the sounds and the way they are combined are unique to a particular area.

White-crowned sparrows are North American songbirds that sometimes develop song "dialects." All the birds in a geographical area sing one version of the species' song, while the birds in a nearby area sing a different version.

A well-known mimic, the mockingbird can fool males of other species by singing copies of their songs.

Bird Mimics

Most young birds learn only the songs of their own species, but there are some exceptions to this rule. A few kinds of birds are **mimics.** They learn other species' songs and include them in their repertoires. The North American mockingbird is one of the best known of these song borrowers. Its scientific name, *Mimus polyglottos,* means "many-tongued mimic." As much as 18 percent of a typical mockingbird repertoire is made up of other birds' songs.

The marsh warbler lives in Europe and nests in wet areas where there is dense vegetation. This species has no songs of its own but copies its whole repertoire from other birds.

Some bird mimics borrow a much larger percentage of their repertoires. The champion is the European marsh warbler, whose *whole* collection of songs seems to be copied from other species. The average marsh warbler mimics about 75 other kinds of birds. Its "teachers" include not only European birds but also species from East Africa, where marsh warblers spend the winter.

Ornithologists are not sure why mockingbirds and other mimics copy the songs of other species. In the case of the marsh warbler, however, there may be a very good explanation. In this species, the adult males do most of their singing during the mating and nesting season. After the young birds hatch from their eggs, the males are mostly silent. A young marsh warbler has little chance to hear adults of its species singing early in its life, when it needs song models to imitate. This may be why it copies the songs of other species.

Like most female songbirds, a female house sparrow makes calls but does not sing.

WHY BIRDS SING

Scientists have a pretty good idea of how birds produce songs and how they learn to sing. The reasons *why* birds sing are not quite so well understood, but one thing is clear. Birdsong is a form of communication. It is a way for birds to send messages and share information with other members of their species.

Singing is one of the two basic ways in which birds use vocal sounds to communicate. The other method is calling.

Bird calls are usually short, simple sounds that send short, simple messages. Some calls warn of danger, for example, the approach of a **predator** (an animal that kills and eats other animals). Contact and recognition calls are used to keep in touch. A female bird calls to her mate to let him know where she is. Young birds exchange calls with their parents so that family members can recognize each other and stay in contact. The young also use calls to ask for food. Young birds need no training to make calls or to recognize them. They are born with these abilities.

Songs are different from calls in many ways. The long training period needed to learn singing is one of these differences. Another is complexity. Bird songs are more complicated than calls, and they are also used to communicate more complex messages.

This male red-winged blackbird uses short, simple calls to keep in touch with his mate.

Playback experiments are often used to study the behavior of wild birds like this fox sparrow.

To find out just what these messages are, ornithologists often use **playback experiments.** In a playback experiment, a researcher takes tape recordings of bird songs out into the field and plays them to see how wild birds react. Do they fly away? Do they start singing themselves? Some scientists use tape players connected to laptop computers. With the help of the computer, they can quickly change the playback to respond to what a bird is doing. For example, they might play the recordings louder or faster or even change to a different song type.

Using these methods, ornithologists have learned a lot about the language of birdsong. They have discovered that most of the "conversations" are about two very important subjects: home and family. A male bird sings to establish his **territory** and to defend this area from other members of his species. A male also uses songs to find a mate.

Defending Territory

Having a territory is vitally important to a male bird. Within this special area, the bird mates, builds a nest, and raises his young. A territory must include good locations for nesting and the right materials for building a nest. It must also have a big enough food supply (seeds, fruits, insects) to feed a growing family.

Top: *Eastern towhees eat berries, and this male has a good supply in his territory.*
Bottom: *Verdins are small desert birds that make their nests out of thorny twigs and grass. A male verdin's territory must include these materials.*

Territories come in many different sizes. Most songbirds and other small birds have small territories no bigger than a few hundred square yards. The territories of large hunting birds such as eagles may be many miles across.

No matter how big or small, a territory is private property for the male bird that lives there. When an American robin, for example, finds a good territory, he establishes his ownership by singing vigorously. He may move from tree to tree or to other "singing posts" within the area. The robin does all this to let other males know that this is *his* home. His song sends the message that he will allow no trespassers.

The "no trespassing" message is in-tended only for other robins. Males of different species usually do not compete over territory. In fact, they often share the same living area. This is because different species eat different foods and also nest in different spots—some high in the trees, others in bushes or beds of reeds.

Playback experiments have shown that singing helps to keep birds of the same species out of an occupied territory. One study done in England during the 1970s involved great tits, a species closely related to North American chickadees. The scientist captured and removed all the male great tits that had territories in one patch of woodland. Then he set up speakers that broadcast recordings of great tit songs in some of the empty territories.

Studies of great tits done in England during the 1970s showed the importance of song in defending a territory.

When males looking for a place to live came to the area, they stayed away from the territories with the broadcast songs. But the birds moved right into the silent territories. It took the newcomers several hours to realize that no real birds were defending any of the territories.

Other playback experiments show what can happen when a male bird enters another male's territory. In these studies, scientists place loudspeakers in an occupied territory and play recordings of the species' songs. When the owner of the territory hears the songs, he usually sings back a challenge. It's as if he is saying, "Get out of my space." If the songs continue to be broadcast, the owner may actually approach the speaker and attack it.

When real birds challenge each other over territory, the conflict doesn't always end in violence. Instead, two males may have a contest in which one bird sings and the other answers with a song. Scientists call this kind of competition **countersinging.**

Countersinging is a kind of endurance contest in which each bird tries to outsing the other. Usually the contestants match each other's songs exactly, but sometimes they change songs. For example, if one bird sings song type A, the other may answer with type B, C, or D. What is the message being sent here? Does the second bird's larger repertoire mean that he will be hard to beat in a competition over territory? No one knows the answer to this question. But scientists have at least one intriguing idea about the role of repertoires in songbird communication.

Three male songbirds communicating in the language of song: an orange-crowned warbler (far left), a black-headed grosbeak (left), and a California gnatcatcher (right)

This theory has been given the nickname **Beau Geste** (BOH JEHST), after a popular book from the 1920s. Beau Geste was a soldier defending a fort from attack. After all his fellow soldiers were killed, he propped their bodies up so that the enemy could see them. Then he ran around firing a gun from their positions to make it seem as if the dead soldiers were still alive and fighting. The trick worked, and the enemy forces gave up their attack on the fort.

If one bird sings many different song variations within a territory, it might have the same effect as Beau Geste's trick. An invader hearing all those songs might believe that the territory is defended by a whole army of birds, not just one. If this theory is correct, then a bird with a larger repertoire than other members of its species would have a real advantage in defending a territory.

Unlike most female songbirds, the female red-winged blackbird sings to defend a territory.

Defending a territory is the job of the male bird in most species. But a few female birds also use song to help keep territories free from intruders. Female red-winged blackbirds and European robins sing for this reason.

Female birds that live in tropical areas are more often singers than their cousins in temperate areas. In these warm regions, many birds—the African robin chat or the bay wren of Central America, for example—often keep the same territories all year around. Males and females stay together for life, and they often sing together to defend their territories. In these amazing duets, each bird in a pair takes turns singing parts of the same song. Their blending is so perfect that it sounds like one bird singing, not two.

Finding a Mate

While a few female birds sing to defend territories, only the males use song for another important purpose: finding a mate. In the United States, Canada, northern Europe, and other areas outside the tropics, this important yearly activity takes place in spring. Many songbirds spend the winter in warm southern climates. Then they return north in spring to find mates and give birth to young.

A brightly colored male cardinal and his not-so-colorful mate. The male's brilliant red feathers help him to attract a female partner.

A male peacock with his train of feathers on display

Male birds are able to mate and reproduce because of the presence of a hormone called **testosterone** (tes-TAHS-tuhr-ohn) in their bodies. (Hormones are chemical substances that cause physical changes in animals.) Testosterone also makes it possible for male birds to sing. A young male begins singing when his body starts producing testosterone during the first year of his life. After he becomes an adult, the level of the hormone in his system increases each spring as the days become longer and the time for mating approaches.

In order to mate and reproduce, a male bird must have two things. One is a good territory. We have already seen how the language of song is used to get and keep a territory. The other thing that a male needs is, of course, a female partner. Song also plays a big role here.

Because getting a mate is so important, male birds have many ways of attracting females. Some males put on elaborate **courtship displays.** They use visual signals to get a female's attention. Peacocks spread their long, beautiful train of feathers. Red-winged blackbirds display the bright red patches on their wings. Other male birds, such as certain species of grouse, perform "dances." They stamp their feet, puff up their feathers, and fan their tails. But for songbirds, singing is probably the most important way that males can attract potential mates.

A male mourning dove (left) does not have bright colors like the cardinal. To attract a female (right), he puffs up the feathers on his throat and sings a cooing song.

Ornithologists have done experiments to find out exactly how females respond to a male's singing. These studies—some done in the field, others in laboratories—have provided interesting results. For one thing, they have shown that songs really work in attracting female birds.

One field experiment involved flycatchers, insect-eating birds found in many parts of the world. Scientists set up nesting boxes and put dummies of male flycatchers in them. In half the boxes, they placed loudspeakers that played flycatcher songs. When female flycatchers came into the area, 9 out of 10 flew to the boxes with the "singing" dummies. The birds showed very little interest in the silent dummies.

An experiment done with female pied flycatchers showed that male birds really do attract mates with their songs.

To study the effect of song on female birds, scientists in Sweden attached tiny radio transmitters to female great reed warblers. These birds make nests in reed beds near bodies of water.

Other researchers have used radio transmitters to study the reaction of female birds to male songs. In Sweden, an ornithologist attached tiny transmitters to some female great reed warblers. These transmitters sent out constant radio signals. By following the signals, the ornithologist tracked the birds as they looked for mates among some males that had territories in a bed of reeds. Each female visited an average of six different territories before she made her final selection. In each case, the lucky male was one that sang a long, complex song from the reed warbler repertoire rather than a short, simple song.

In choosing mates, the female great reed warblers seemed to prefer males that put on a more elaborate singing performance than their rivals. Other studies show that females of many species are attracted by good performers. They also seem to find large repertoires appealing. In one study, captive female song sparrows heard tapes of male song sparrows singing. The female birds paid much more attention to the males that sang 8 different song types than to those that sang 4. The males with 16 song types in their repertoires were a really big hit.

Why would a male that sings a long complicated song or has a large repertoire be so attractive to a female bird looking for a mate? Suppose she chooses this male over another that doesn't give such a good performance. Will it make any real difference to her or to her young? Or is the male bird's fancy singing just a form of advertising, like a television commercial that uses bright colors and catchy tunes to sell cars?

Birdsong can be seen as a kind of advertising, but the messages that male birds send may be more "truthful" than the average car commercial. Scientific research seems to show that good singers do make better partners, at least when it comes to reproduction.

The songs of both the rose-breasted grosbeak (top) and the scarlet tanager (bottom) *have been compared to the robin's song. According to some bird guides, a male grosbeak sounds like a robin that has had singing lessons, while the tanager sounds like a robin with a sore throat.*

The female rose-breasted grosbeak (top) and scarlet tanager (bottom) *have no problem recognizing their own species' songs. They can even pick out the singer that gives the best performance.*

A male bird that sings long songs rather than short ones may be indirectly communicating important information about himself. It takes a lot of energy to sing a long song unbroken by pauses. A male that sings in this way is probably strong and healthy. He is also well fed, since he doesn't have to stop singing very often to look for food. This suggests that his territory contains a good food supply and that he does a good job of collecting it. All these things would make him an excellent choice as a mate and a father to a female bird's young.

A large repertoire may also send a message about a male's qualities and the territory he lives in. Older birds often know more song types than young beginners. They may also be stronger, more experienced at raising young, and more able to defend a territory against invaders. A female that hears many different song types from one male singer may be getting an important message: this male has all the basic qualities needed in a mate.

THE LANGUAGE OF SONG

The sound of birds singing is such a familiar part of most people's daily lives that we don't give it much thought. The song of the chickadee or the cardinal is simply background music to our outdoor activities or a wake-up call that comes much too early in the morning. But we have learned that bird songs are so much more than this. They are communications that are vitally important in the lives of birds.

So the next time you hear a black-capped chickadee singing *"FEE-bee"* *"FEE-bee"* or the *"Birdy, birdy, birdy"* of a cardinal, stop and think about the message in the song.

The eastern towhee used to be a common bird in the northeastern United States, but its numbers have dropped sharply in recent years.

SONGBIRDS IN DANGER

In many parts of the United States, bird songs are not heard as often as they were in years past. This change has been particularly noticeable in the woodlands and forests of the eastern United States. Studies have shown that the numbers of warblers, wood thrushes, and some other small songbirds have been declining in these areas since the 1980s. What is happening to the beautiful forest singers?

Scientists think that the songbirds have been affected by changes in the woodland environments where they live. Most of the threatened species migrate to spend the winter in Central America and South America. In these areas, forests are being cut down and replaced with crops such as coffee and bananas. Without forests to provide shelter and food, the birds have problems finding winter homes.

Woodland songbirds also face a changed environment when they come north to mate and have their young. The large forests where they usually nest are disappearing from the eastern half of the United States. They are being replaced by forest fragments—small patches of woodland often surrounded by farm fields or suburban housing developments.

Female cowbirds lay their eggs in the nests of other birds, including those of many small songbirds. Some songbirds do not recognize that cowbird eggs are different from their own eggs. They provide equal care for all. But cowbird chicks usually hatch earlier than young songbirds, and they are much larger. The small parent birds have a hard time feeding both these hungry outsiders and their own young. The cowbirds usually survive, but the young songbirds often die from lack of food.

A female brown-headed cowbird

Songbirds nesting in forest fragments face many threats. Snakes and raccoons are much more common in such areas than in the deep forest. These predators eat both bird eggs and young birds. An even bigger threat is the brown-headed cowbird, which is also common in small patches of woodland.

This wood thrush nest contains three bright blue thrush eggs and two cowbird eggs.

Some bird species, for example, American robins, are able to recognize cowbird eggs and push them out of their nests. But most forest songbirds do not have this skill because they have only recently become victims of cowbirds. Until these species can learn to defend themselves against the intruders, they will be at risk. This threat, added to the other dangers of nesting in forest fragments, means that the populations of some songbirds will probably continue to decline.

Can anything be done to prevent the loss of these woodland singers? We can make a start right at home by preserving the large areas of forest that are still left in the United States. Federal and state agencies protect some forests. National conservation organizations such as the Nature Conservancy help in the effort by purchasing forest lands and keeping them safe from development. These may be small steps, but at least they will provide a safe nesting place for some threatened songbirds.

The wood thrush is one of the most threatened American songbirds. The population of wood thrushes in some areas has been declining steadily since the late 1970s.

GLOSSARY

Beau Geste theory: the idea that a bird with more songs in his repertoire than others of his species might be more successful in defending a territory

bronchi: the two main tubes that connect the windpipe to the lungs

calls: short, simple sounds used by birds to keep in touch or to communicate warnings

countersinging: a "contest" in which one male bird sings and another answers with a song

courtship displays: actions or behaviors used by male birds to attract females

frequency: the number of sound waves passing a certain point in one second of time

mimics: birds that learn the songs of other species and include them in their repertoires

ornithologists: scientists who study the biology and the behavior of birds

oscines: songbirds, members of the scientific suborder Oscines

passerines: birds with feet adapted for perching. Passerines have three toes pointing forward and one backward.

playback experiments: scientific experiments in which tape-recorded bird songs are played back in a natural setting to test the response of wild birds

predator: an animal that kills other animals for food

repertoire: the collection of song types sung by an individual bird or a species

song types: different versions of a species' basic song

sonograph: an electronic device that analyzes sound waves and displays the results in **sonograms**

species: a group of animals that have many common characteristics. Species is one of the main categories in the scientific system of classification.

syrinx: the sound-producing organ in birds

template: a pattern or guide used to shape something. Scientists use the word to describe a bird's inborn knowledge of its species' songs.

territory: the area in which an animal finds food and raises its young

testosterone: a hormone that makes it possible for male animals to mate and reproduce. This chemical also gives male birds the ability to sing.

INDEX

bay wren, 34
Beau Geste theory, 33
blue jay, 9
bronchi, 19
brown thrasher, 14, 15

calls, 8, 10, 27
cardinal, 7, 9, 14, 35
chaffinch, 20–21
chickadee, black-capped, 7, 9, 30
chipping sparrow, 15, 17
communication, birdsong as, 27, 28, 30, 31, 32, 40–41, 42
countersinging, 32
courtship displays, 36
cowbird, brown-headed, 44–45

dialects, song, 23

female birds: calls used by, 10, 27; and defense of territory, 34, 35; response of, to male songs, 38–41
flycatcher, 38
forest fragments, 43–44, 45
frequency, sound, 12, 21

great reed warbler, 39
great tit, 30–31

male birds: learning to sing, 19–23; using song to defend territories, 28–34, 36; using song to find mates, 35–41
marsh warbler, 25
mating, 29; role of song in, 35, 36–41
meadowlark, western, 16
mimics, 24–25
mockingbird, 14, 18, 24

nightingale, 14, 16–17

ornithologists, 8, 10, 11, 13, 23, 25; research of, 20–21, 28, 30–31, 38–39
oscines, 8
ovenbird, 15, 17

passerines, 8
playback experiments, 28, 30, 31
predators, 27, 44

red-winged blackbird, 27, 34, 36
repertoire, 24–25, 40; size of, 15, 16, 17, 32–33, 39, 41
robin: American, 9, 30, 45; European, 34
robin chat, 34

song sparrow, 22, 39
song type, 14, 15, 17, 32, 39
sonogram, 12–13, 14, 16, 21
sonograph, 12–13
sound waves, 12, 18
syrinx, 18–19

tape recorder, used in studying songbirds, 11–12, 28
template, 22
territory, 28, 29, 41; size of, 30; song used to defend, 30–34, 36
testosterone, 36
threats to songbirds, 43–45

white-crowned sparrow, 21, 23
wood thrush, 7, 43, 44, 45

ABOUT THE AUTHOR

Sylvia A. Johnson has had a long and productive career as an editor and writer of books for young people. She has worked on publications about such diverse subjects as a beekeeper and his bees, life in a wolf pack, and the role of maps in human history.

In her years as an editor, Ms. Johnson has collaborated with writers in the fields of archaeology, botany, behavioral biology, and many other fascinating subjects. Doing research for her own books, she has studied rare old maps, observed surgery on injured raptors, and donned a bee suit and veiled hat to get a close-up look at a beekeeper at work.

Sylvia A. Johnson makes her home in Minneapolis, where she lives in a gray-shingled house with Smokey, a small but dignified gray-striped cat.

The photographs in this book are reproduced through the courtesy of: © Tom Vezo, pp. 2, 4–5, 6–7, 9 (both), 10, 18, 20 (inset), 23, 26, 29 (top), 30, 32 (left), 34, 35, 40 (both), 41 (both), 42, 43, 44 (left); © Charles W. Melton, pp. 8, 14, 15, 16, 28, 29 (bottom), 32 (right), 33, 45; © Tim Gallagher, p. 11; © Roger Wilmshurst/The National Audubon Society Collection/Photo Researchers, Inc., pp. 17, 20, 31, 39; © Tom J. Ulrich, pp. 22, 36; © Steve Bentsen, pp. 24, 27; © Alan Williams/Natural History Photographic Agency, p. 25; © Laura Elaine Moore, p. 37; © John Hawkins; Frank Lane Picture Agency/CORBIS, p. 38; © Todd Fink/Daybreak Imagery, p. 44 (right).

Front cover: © Tom Vezo
Back cover: © Steve Bentsen

Sonograms on pages 13 and 21 reprinted from "Bird Song Learning: Causes and Consequences," by P. B. J. Slater, in *Ethology, Ecology, and Evolution* Vol. 1, No. 1, pp. 19–46, with permission of the publisher.